wh

Carey Molter

ABDO
Publishing Company

Published by SandCastle™, an imprint of ABDO Publishing Company, 4940 Viking Drive, Edina, Minnesota 55435.

Printed in the United States.

Cover and interior photo credits: Artville, Digital Vision, Eyewire Images, FPG International, PhotoDisc.

Library of Congress Cataloging-in-Publication Data

Molter, Carey, 1973-
    Wh / Carey Molter.
        p. cm. -- (Blends)
    Includes index.
    ISBN 1-57765-410-2
        1. Readers (Primary) [1. English language--Phonetics.] I. Title. II. Blends (Series)

PE1119 .M653 2000
428.1--dc21

00-033205

The SandCastle concept, content, and reading method have been reviewed and approved by a national advisory board including literacy specialists, librarians, elementary school teachers, early childhood education professionals, and parents.

Let Us Know

After reading the book, SandCastle would like you to tell us your stories about reading. What is your favorite page? Was there something hard that you needed help with? Share the ups and downs of learning to read. We want to hear from you! To get posted on the Abdo Publishing Company Web site, send us email at:

sandcastle@abdopub.com

About SandCastle™
Nonfiction books for the beginning reader

- Basic concepts of phonics are incorporated with integrated language methods of reading instruction. Most words are short, and phrases, letter sounds, and word sounds are repeated.

- Readability is determined by the number of words in each sentence, the number of characters in each word, and word lists based on curriculum frameworks.

- Full-color photography reinforces word meanings and concepts.

- "Words I Can Read" list at the end of each book teaches basic elements of grammar, helps the reader recognize the words in the text, and builds vocabulary.

- Reading levels are indicated by the number of flags on the castle.

Look for more SandCastle books in these three reading levels:

Level 1 (one flag)	**Level 2** (two flags)	**Level 3** (three flags)

Grades Pre-K to K 5 or fewer words per page	**Grades K to 1** 5 to 10 words per page	**Grades 1 to 2** 10 to 15 words per page

wh

Whitby is the girl who always has fun.

wh

Whitley gets ready to whack the ball.

He likes tennis.

wh

Whitman whispers a secret while I giggle.

wh

Whitney loves
whipped cream
on her treat.

wh

We think whoever
rides in a
wheelbarrow is silly.

wh

We play in the whirlpool.

The water whooshes around us.

My pinwheel is neat.
It whirls in the breeze.

wh

I get dizzy when I do cartwheels.

This is fun.

wh

What do I help my mom fix?

(wheel)

21

Words I Can Read

Nouns

A noun is a person, place, or thing

ball (BAWL) p. 7
breeze (BREEZ) p. 17
cream (KREEM) p. 11
fun (FUHN) p. 5
girl (GUHRL) p. 5
mom (MOM) p. 21
pinwheel (PIN-weel) p. 17
secret (SEE-krit) p. 9

tennis (TEN-iss) p. 7
treat (TREET) p. 11
water (WAW-tur) p. 15
wheel (WEEL) p. 21
wheelbarrow (WEEL-ba-roh) p. 13
whirlpool (WURL-pool) p. 15

Plural Nouns

A plural noun is more than one person, place, or thing

cartwheels (KART-weelz) p. 19

Proper Nouns

A proper noun is the name of a person, place, or thing

Whitby (WIT-bee) p. 5
Whitley (WIT-lee) p. 7

Whitman (WIT-man) p. 9
Whitney (WIT-nee) p. 11

Verbs
A verb is an action or being word

do (DOO) pp. 19, 21
fix (FIKSS) p. 21
get (GET) p. 19
gets (GETSS) p. 7
giggle (GIG-uhl) p. 9
has (HAZ) p. 5
help (HELP) p. 21
is (IZ) pp. 5, 13, 17, 19
likes (LIKESS) p. 7

loves (LUHVZ) p. 11
play (PLAY) p. 15
rides (RIDEZ) p. 13
think (THINGK) p. 13
whack (WAK) p. 7
whirls (WURLZ) p. 17
whispers (WISS-purz) p. 9
whooshes (WOOSH-ez) p. 15

Adjectives
An adjective describes something

dizzy (DIZ-ee) p. 19
her (HUR) p. 11
fun (FUHN) p. 19
my (MEY) p. 17, 21

neat (NEET) p. 17
ready (RED-ee) p. 7
silly (SIL-ee) p. 13
whipped (WIPT) p. 11

Match these wh Words to the Pictures

whale

whisk

wheat

wheelchair

24